Coca-Cola 600

by Eric Ethan

Gareth Stevens Publishing
MILWAUKEE

The author wishes to thank Glen Fitzgerald, George Philips, Mary Jo Lindahl, and Juanita Jones for their help and encouragement.

For a free color catalog describing Gareth Stevens Publishing's list of high-quality books and multimedia programs, call 1-800-542-2595 (USA) or 1-800-461-9120 (Canada). Gareth Stevens Publishing's Fax: (414) 225-0377.

Library of Congress Cataloging-in-Publication Data

Ethan, Eric.
  Coca-Cola 600 / by Eric Ethan.
    p. cm. — (NASCAR! an imagination library series)
  Includes index.
  Summary: Discusses the background, events, and rules of the Coca-Cola 600, the longest automobile race sanctioned by NASCAR.
    ISBN 0-8368-2137-8 (lib. bdg.)
  1. Coca-Cola 600 (Automobile race)—Juvenile literature. [1. Coca-Cola 600 (Automobile race). 2. Stock car racing.] I. Title. II. Series: Ethan, Eric. NASCAR! an imagination library series.
  GV1033.5.C63E85   1999
  796.72'06'875676—dc21   99-14716

First published in North America in 1999 by
Gareth Stevens Publishing
1555 North RiverCenter Drive, Suite 201
Milwaukee, WI 53212 USA

This edition © 1999 by Gareth Stevens, Inc. Text by Eric Ethan. Photographs © 1998: p. 19 - CIA Stock; Cover, pp. 7, 11, 13, 15, 17, 21 - Don Grassman; p. 5 - Sammy Kosh. Illustration: p. 9 - The Official NASCAR Preview and Press Guide. Additional end matter © 1999 by Gareth Stevens, Inc.

Text: Eric Ethan
Page layout: Lesley M. White
Cover design: Lesley M. White
Editorial assistant: Diane Laska

Printed in the United States of America

1 2 3 4 5 6 7 8 9 03 02 01 00 99

TABLE OF CONTENTS

Metric Chart
1 mile = 1.609 kilometers
100 miles = 160.9 km
600 miles = 965.4 km

Words that appear in the glossary are printed in
boldface type the first time they occur in the text.

THE COCA-COLA 600

The Coca-Cola 600 is the longest race **sanctioned** by the National Association for **Stock Car** Auto Racing (NASCAR). Joe Lee Johnson won the first Coca-Cola 600 in 1960 with an average speed of 107.5 miles per hour. The race lasted almost six hours! That is a very long time to drive at high speed.

Since 1960, twenty different drivers have won this race. Some of the most famous NASCAR drivers have won the Coca-Cola 600 more than once. Legendary driver Darrell Waltrip has won this grueling race five times. In 1996, Dale Jarrett won it for the first time. His average speed was 147.5 miles per hour. Today's NASCAR racers go much faster than they did in 1960. Even so, the race still took Jarrett 4½ hours to complete.

The Charlotte Motor Speedway in North Carolina is home to the Coca-Cola 600.
CIA Stock Photo: Sammy Kosh

CHARLOTTE MOTOR SPEEDWAY

The Coca-Cola 600 is held in late May each year at the Charlotte Motor Speedway near Concord, North Carolina. Since 1999, the track's new name is Lowe's Motor Speedway. The speedway is called the "Mecca of Motor Sports" because it is built to give racing fans a great view and plenty of comfort. Over 165,000 people crowd the stands on race day, resulting in the largest attendance of any track in the United States.

The racetrack is a 1½-mile **oval**. The turns are steeply **banked**. This means that the outer part of the corner is tilted up so the road surface leans to the inside. This helps the cars go around the corners at high speed without flying off the track.

Cars on the left head into a pit lane, which is flat. Cars on the right continue on the banked racecourse.
CIA Stock Photo: Don Grassman

THE TRACK

Average track speeds have steadily climbed since the first race. A record of 151.952 miles per hour was set in 1995 by Bobby Labonte. The single-lap record was set by Ward Burton in 1994. He completed one lap in 29 seconds at a speed of 185.759 miles per hour.

Top race and **qualifying** speeds are higher at other NASCAR courses. Short **straightaways** at Charlotte hold speeds down. Drivers go faster when they are driving a single qualifying lap in order to get a good starting position. Driving an entire race at high speeds, especially one that lasts as long as the Coca-Cola 600, would be too hard on a car's motor. Cars would break down before the race was over. To win a NASCAR race, you must finish it — not just go fast.

A track diagram shows the small bends in the seating along the main straightaway at Charlotte. This gives the crowd a better view.
The Official NASCAR Preview and Press Guide

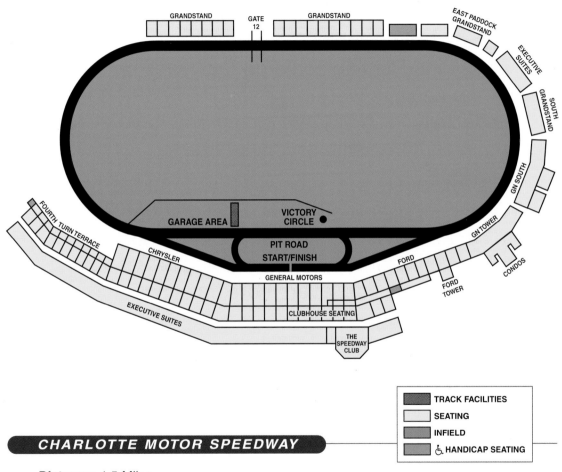

GRANDSTAND   GATE 12   GRANDSTAND   EAST PADDOCK GRANDSTAND

EXECUTIVE SUITES

SOUTH GRANDSTAND

GN SOUTH

GN TOWER

CONDOS

FORD TOWER

FORD

GENERAL MOTORS

CHRYSLER

FOURTH TURN TERRACE

EXECUTIVE SUITES

CLUBHOUSE SEATING

THE SPEEDWAY CLUB

GARAGE AREA   VICTORY CIRCLE

PIT ROAD START/FINISH

TRACK FACILITIES

SEATING

INFIELD

♿ **HANDICAP SEATING**

CHARLOTTE MOTOR SPEEDWAY

Distance: *1.5 Miles*

Banking: *24 degrees*

Qualifying Record: *Ward Burton, 185.759 mph (29.07 seconds), set October 6, 1994*

Race Record (600 Miles): *Bobby Labonte, 151.952 mph, set May 28, 1995*

NASCAR RACERS

NASCAR race cars have changed a lot since the first race in 1948. Back then, regular cars from Ford, Chevrolet, and Pontiac could do fairly well on the track if the engines were big enough. Today, cars are built especially for NASCAR racing and have almost nothing in common with ordinary cars.

NASCAR racers are specially built from the ground up. Tires cost over $1,300 for a set of four. Race car teams can use over a dozen sets qualifying for and running a single race. The frame, engine, and body panels for the car cost even more, making NASCAR racing a very expensive sport. Prize money helps cover some of the costs. More money comes in from **sponsors** that put their **logos** on the cars.

Jeff Gordon, sponsored by Du Pont, won the 1998 Coca-Cola 600 race.
CIA Stock Photo: Don Grassman

11

Race cars are built for speed and strength. Team mechanics also want cars that are easy to work on. Motors are usually changed right after a car qualifies for a race. Drivers want to use a fresh motor for race day, not one that was run full-out to qualify.

Car designers try to put important working parts in the places where they will be protected. Cooling systems for oil and water can be easily damaged. If that happens, the car quickly stops running. Cooling radiators are surrounded by a welded steel tube frame. If the driver hits another car or the outside wall, this frame absorbs some of the damage. If the damage is not too bad, the driver can stay in the race.

Mark Martin leads the pack into the first turn at the 1998 Coca-Cola 600.
CIA Stock Photo: Don Grassman

DRIVERS AND TEAMS

Dale Earnhardt drives car number three for the GM Goodwrench Team. The car is owned by Richard Childress. As owner, it is Childress's job to find the best drivers and build a team of mechanics and a **pit crew** that will help his car win. Car racing is very challenging both on the track and off. Enormous amounts of money are needed to pay personnel and build winning race cars from the ground up.

Earnhardt has been a champion NASCAR driver for many years. He ran his first NASCAR race as a professional in 1975. Since that time, he has won over $30 million for various teams.

Dale Earnhardt speeds down the track during qualifying at the Charlotte Motor Speedway in 1998.
CIA Stock Photo: Don Grassman

QUALIFYING

Two days before the race, drivers practice on the course until they are ready to go full speed on a qualifying lap. Team mechanics use this time to tune their car to the track. This is a very important part of qualifying well and winning the race. On NASCAR race cars, mechanics can change the suspension and steering so it is just right for a particular course. Drivers test each of the changes on the track until the driver and mechanics think they have the car just right. Then the driver takes the car around the track as fast as possible during his qualifying lap. The fastest drivers get to start the race in the front rows. Races are won or lost by what mechanics do to the car in the pits as much as by what the driver does on the track.

Darkness descends before the 600-mile Coca-Cola 600 race ends.
CIA Stock Photo: Don Grassman

RACE DAY

Drivers line up for the race in the order in which they qualified. The fastest qualifying car sits in the **pole position**. This is the inside position in the first row. Cars begin circling the track in this starting order, waiting for the **starter** to drop the green flag. When that happens, the cars all accelerate and try to get in front.

Drivers then start to settle in on the track and look for the groove. The groove is the very best path on the track surface for cars to go quickly through the turns and back onto the straightaway.

Champion drivers have very smooth driving styles. All of them can drive very fast, but they know finishing the race is the key to winning. They don't want to go through their fuel too quickly or damage their motors by pushing too hard.

After qualifying, team mechanics look over their car and give the "okay" that it is ready to race.
CIA Stock Photo

19

PIT CREWS

At some point during the race, all cars have to make pit stops for gas, new tires, and, sometimes, repairs. Pit crews work very quickly to get their team's car in and out of the pit as fast as possible. Seconds count during a race.

Sometimes cars hit each other or the wall during a race. Mechanics try to fix whatever they can to get a car back onto the track. Dents on the sides of the car usually aren't a problem on shorter tracks like the Charlotte Motor Speedway. Speeds are low enough that losing a smooth body panel doesn't cause too much of a problem. On tracks over two miles, however, even minor dents and damage can slow a car enough on the straightaways to lose the race.

Driver Ernie Irvan's pit crew changes tires lightning fast during the 1998 Coca-Cola 600.
CIA Stock Photo: Don Grassman

21

ACCIDENTS AND SAFETY

When NASCAR first began, drivers wore only a seat belt and sometimes a helmet. Today, safety is a science. Drivers wear special **fire-retardant** clothing. Helmets are greatly improved over the originals and contain emergency air tubes in case the car fills with smoke. A strong harness holds the driver tightly in his seat. Padded roll cages made of welded steel tubing surround the driver.

Unfortunately, accidents do happen in NASCAR racing. They are an unavoidable part of the sport. The goal of modern safety science is to help drivers survive accidents with the least injury possible. Many famous drivers have walked away unharmed from collisions that totally destroyed their cars.

GLOSSARY

You can find these words on the pages listed. Reading a word in a sentence helps you understand it even better.

banked — inclined upward from the inside edge 6, 9

fire-retardant (ree-TAR-dent) — resistant to fire 22

logos (LOW-gos) — graphic designs that feature the name or product of a company 10

oval (OH-val) — a shape or figure that looks like an egg or an ellipse 6

pit crew — a team of workers that maintains a race car off the track 14, 20

pole position — the inside, front spot in a car race 18

qualifying (KWAH-lih-fy-ing) — a test that makes a person or object fit for a certain position 8, 12, 14, 16, 18

sanctioned (SANK-shunned) — approved by an official group 4

sponsors (SPON-sers) — businesses that financially support something 10

starter — a person who signals the beginning of a race 18

stock car — a new-model sedan manufactured by Detroit automakers, such as Ford, General Motors, and Chevrolet 4

straightaways — the straight parts of a roadway in a racecourse 8, 18, 20

PLACES TO WRITE

International Motor Sports Museum
Public Relations Manager
3198 Speedway Boulevard
Talladega, AL 35160

Daytona USA
Public Relations Manager
1801 West International Boulevard
Daytona Beach, FL 32114

Motorbooks International
Public Relations Manager
729 Prospect Avenue/Box 1
Osceola, WI 54020

Lowe's Motor Speedway
(formerly Charlotte Motor Speedway)
P.O. Box 600
Concord, NC 28026

WEB SITES

www.nascar.com

This is the official web site of the National Association for Stock Car Auto Racing.

www.ciastockphoto.com

This is one of the best NASCAR photo sites. It is the source of many of the pictures in this book. It presents new images during each racing season.

racing.yahoo.com/rac/nascar

At this web site, race fans can find current NASCAR race results, standings, schedules, driver profiles, feature stories, and merchandise.

Due to the dynamic nature of the Internet, some web sites stay current longer than others. To find additional web sites, use a reliable search engine with one or more of the following keywords: *Charlotte Motor Speedway, Coca-Cola 600, Dale Earnhardt, Jeff Gordon, Bobby Labonte, Mark Martin, NASCAR,* and *Darrell Waltrip.*

INDEX